D0417193

RD CITY AND COUNTY
WITHDRAWN
LIBRARIES

LOOK AND SAY
WHAT YOU SEE
IN THE TOWN

For Naomi, Elijah,
Ben and Joey.

S.B.

First published in 2018 by Nosy Crow Ltd
The Crow's Nest, 14 Baden Place, Crosby Row
London SE1 1YW
www.nosycrow.com

ISBN 978 0 85763 943 1

'The National Trust' and the oak leaf logo are registered trademarks of The National Trust (Enterprises) Limited (a subsidiary
of The National Trust for Places of Historic Interest or Natural Beauty, Registered Charity Number 205846).

Nosy Crow and associated logos are trademarks and/or registered
trademarks of Nosy Crow Ltd (Registered Company Number 7130282).

Text © Nosy Crow 2018
Illustrations © Sebastien Braun 2018

The right of Nosy Crow to be identified as the author and Sebastien Braun
to be identified as the illustrator of this work has been asserted.

All rights reserved

This book is sold subject to the condition that it shall not, by way of trade or otherwise,
be lent, hired out or otherwise circulated in any form of binding or cover other than that in which it is published.
No part of this publication may be reproduced, stored in a retrieval system, or transmitted in any form or by any means
(electronic, mechanical, photocopying, recording or otherwise) without the prior written permission of Nosy Crow Ltd.

A CIP catalogue record for this book is available from the British Library.

Printed in Turkey

Papers used by Nosy Crow are made from wood grown in sustainable forests.

1 3 5 7 9 8 6 4 2

Look and Say
WHAT YOU SEE
IN THE TOWN

LEABHARLANN PHORT LÁIRGE	
Bertrams	19/04/2018
UK	02325219

Sebastien Braun

nosy crow

There's plenty of wildlife to be found in the town.
People often visit ponds to feed the ducks.

Can you
see . . .?

duck   duckling   water lily   Canada goose

Ducks like to eat birdseed, oats and vegetable trimmings.

Can you see any baby animals?

boat

moorhen

car

frog

bin

Today is market day and there are many colourful stalls selling fruit, vegetables and flowers.

Can you see . . . ?

 radishes

 carrots

 shopping basket

 sunflowers

What would you like to
buy at the market?

potatoes

pineapples

apples

bananas

sandwich board sign

Do you have a garden? What do you do there? People sometimes grow their own vegetables in their gardens.

Watch out for slugs though – they love to munch lettuce!

Can you see . . . ?

 bumblebee

 magpie

 lettuce

 wheelbarrow

snail   strawberries   trowel   slug   watering can

Towns usually have parks — they are a great place to take a dog for a walk or play in the playground.

Can you see . . . ?

 bench

 dog

 helmet

 squirrel

What do you like doing at the park?

tree   scooter   tulips   football   swing

Down by the canal you'll see a lot of boats.
Long, flat boats like these are called barges.

Can you
see . . . ?

 dragonfly

 vole

 life ring

 heron

Canals are a great place to
spot wildlife. Look out for
water birds and plants, too!

swan

rabbit

pot plant

barge

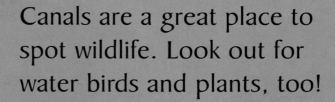

bullrushes

Some towns are close to the sea and you can walk along the seafront.

Gallery

Fish & Chips

Can you see . . . ?

kayak  seal  surfboard  lighthouse

How many seagulls
can you count?

 statue  dolphin   seagull   kite   ice cream van

It's busy in the town centre – there's always so much going on!

Can you see . . . ?

 cup of tea

 pigeon

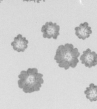 blossom

 menu

On a sunny day, it can be
nice to sit outside and
watch people go past.

 bicycle

 signpost

 scooter

 poster

 fountain

Some animals are nocturnal and only come out when it's dark, so the streets can be full of wildlife – even when you're asleep!

Can you see . . .?

 cat

 bat

 moth

 little owl

What can you see
hiding in the dark?

tawny owl

moon

fox

hedgehog streetlight

On the high street, there are shops selling all sorts of wonderful things. Which shop would you like to go into?

Can you see . . .?

 butterfly

 book

 puppy

 starling

Have you ever been on a bus?

BAKERY

FRUIT & VEG

teddy bear   bus stop   aeroplane   bread   pushchair

A village is smaller than a town and there are often farms nearby.

Can you see any farm animals?

Can you see . . . ?

picnic   cow   hot-air balloon   tractor

church   bus   horse rider   sheep   kestrel

Even when it's raining, you can have plenty of fun outside.

Can you see . . . ?

 wellies

conkers

hat

 tricycle

You can put on your wellies and
go splashing in the puddles!

 umbrella

 raincoat

 puddle

 crow

autumn leaves

In the winter, it can be hard for birds to find food, so it's good to put birdseed out for them.

Can you see . . .?

snowdrop   robin   bird feeder   shed

How many types of
bird can you spot
on the bird table?

ivy   blue tit   mouse   blackbird   birdhouse